To: Ayani Cook

From: _[signature]_

Ayani, keep reading and believing in golden opportunities that's going to come your way..... you're a very special person and my little friend!!

023

SEEING MOMMY
ALL DAY LONG

Vincent A. Pendarvis

Illustrated by: Hatice Bayramoglu

Seeing Mommy All Day Long

Copyright © 2021 by Vincent A. Pendarvis

Illustrated by: Hatice Bayramoglu

ISBN 978-0-5789-1186-1

Published by: Indy Pub

Early Morning in My Apartment

Crack, crack, crack! I could hear eggs breaking. The sweet smell of bacon filled the air. That was the way most mornings started in my apartment.

"Everybody up! Everybody up! Everybody up!" my mother called.

I was the oldest of three, and Mommy always woke me first.

4

"Alex, make sure you wash your face and brush your hair. And don't forget to brush your teeth!" she would say. Mommy wanted me up first so I could help my brother and sister get ready while she cooked breakfast. I liked helping Mommy do things around the house.

I lived in a one-room apartment in the city with my mother, brother, and sister. My brother and sister were too young to go to school. Sometimes when Mommy was at work, we would stay with Mrs. Jones, who lived down the hall.

Mommy worked at the hospital around the corner. Mommy did her best to make sure we had all the things we needed—and some extras just for fun. That's why I liked to help her. To me, she was the greatest mommy ever!

It was the start of a new school year. I was starting third grade in a brand-new school. I was nervous and excited, and something about the day felt very strange to me. Somehow I knew this day would be *very* different from any other day.

On the Way to the Bus Stop

After breakfast, I kissed and hugged Mommy and told her that I loved her. I said goodbye to my brother and sister. Then I grabbed my book bag. I was off to school!

Before I could reach the door, Mommy said, "Be careful, and don't get into any trouble!"

"Yes ma'am," I replied. A question popped into my head. *Why did Mommy say that? She knows I don't get into trouble!*

Near the elevator, I saw Mrs. Jones, who was on her way to pick up my brother and sister. She was like a grandmother to all the kids in the apartment building. Mrs. Jones would give us peppermint sticks that melted in our mouths. When it was hot, she gave us strawberry ice cream. It was better than any of the ice cream from any of the shops for miles and miles around. All we had to do to get a treat was to show good manners to her and the other grown-ups in our building. When she saw you doing that, she would load you up with goodies!

"Good morning, Mrs. Jones," I said.

"Good morning, Alex," she replied. Then she reached into her apron pocket and gave me a sweet peppermint stick.

"Thank you, Mrs. Jones," I said while shaking her hand.

"First day back to school?" she asked.

"Yes ma'am," I said. "It's a new school, Mrs. Jones, and I'm a little nervous."

"It's okay to be nervous on the first day, but as the day goes on, that nervousness will go away," she said.

Ding! The elevator doors slid open.

"Alex, make sure you watch your fingers in those elevator doors," said Mrs. Jones. "Have a good day, and try not to get into any trouble!"

"Yes ma'am," I replied. As I rode the elevator to the lobby, I thought, *Hmm. That's just what Mommy would say!*

As I walked out the door of the apartment building, I saw one of Mommy's friends with her daughters, who are twins.

"Good morning, Alex," she said.

"Good morning, Ms. Simpkins. Good morning, girls," I said.

I'm taking the twins over to your old school, Alex. Have a good day at your new school, and try not to get into any trouble!"

"Yes ma'am, Ms. Simpkins. I won't!" *Not again*, I thought. *That's just what Mommy would say!*

Mrs. Baxter's Store

10

I stopped at the corner store and headed straight to the candy aisle. I chose two pieces of candy and an extra pencil. Then I heard a voice coming from the back.

"Alex, is that you?" It was Mrs. Baxter, the store owner.

I said, "Yes ma'am. It's me."

Mrs. Baxter had been running the store since my mommy was a little girl, and she was always nice to me and my friends. She would give you an extra cookie even if you didn't have enough money. She was just that kind!

At the cash register, she noticed that my pants were hanging too low. "Alex, pull your pants up," she said. "You can't go to school on your first day with your pants hanging off you!"

"Yes ma'am," I said. I thought to myself, *Not again. That's just what Mommy would say!*

Mrs. **Baxter** leaned over to me and said with a smile, "Now, hurry up and pay for that candy so you won't miss your bus for school!" I quickly gave her some coins and dashed out the door.

14

Arriving at My New School

After hustling to the bus stop, I arrived—and not a minute too soon. Along came the school bus! I wanted a good seat, so I jumped in front of some kids who were talking and not paying attention to the line.

Then from out of nowhere, the bus driver, Ms. O'Keefe, spotted me and yelled, "Boy, if you know what I know, you'll get back to the end of that line!" Then she recognized me. "Aren't you Ms. Beverly's son, Alex?"

I replied, "Yes ma'am."

"I saw your mother at the store shopping for school supplies," she said. "She asked me to watch out for you and make sure you don't get into trouble."

I turned around, as I was told to, and went to the back of the line. I was the very last to get on the bus. I got the worst seat in the back. What a bummer that was!

Then—finally—we arrived at school. As I started to get off the bus, Ms. O'Keefe stopped me. "Alex, you make sure you do as you're told, and don't get into any trouble!"

"Yes ma'am," I replied.

16

The bus attendant, Ms. Oliver, greeted us as we stepped off the bus. "Make sure you stay in line on your way to breakfast in the cafeteria," she said.

I had already had one breakfast, but the sweet smell of cinnamon rolls made me want to eat again!

Now it was my turn to pass Ms. Oliver as we walked in a straight line.

"Hey, aren't you Ms. Beverly's boy?" she asked. "Your name is Alex, right?"

"Yes ma'am," I said.

"I was told to watch out for you and make sure you don't get into any trouble!"

"Oh, no ma'am. No trouble from me!" I said.

When we got to the cafeteria, the lunchroom ladies started talking. They were looking straight at me! One of them was my mommy's friend Ms. Russell, who walked up to me and said, "Alex, you come over here and get in my line!" she laughed. "Your mama said to make sure you were well fed. She also said for me to keep an eye on you and make sure you don't get into any trouble."

"Yes ma'am," I replied.

Surprises at the New School

With my belly full from breakfast, thanks to Ms. Russell, I hurried off to my homeroom.

Ring, ring, went the first bell.

I ran down the hall to make sure I got to class before the second bell.

Then I heard a voice. "No running in the hallways!" It was Mrs. Harrison.

Wait a minute! What? Mrs. Harrison was a teacher from my *old* school! What was she doing here? Then I remembered something from the year before. On the last day of school, she'd made an announcement. She was going to a new school to be closer to her home and her sick mother.

"Alex, is that you?" she asked.

"Yes ma'am," I said.

"Your name is on my class list. I will be your music teacher! I will be so excited to see you later in my class."

As I turned toward my homeroom, I heard her say something else. "I had a talk with your mother yesterday," she said. "Your mother asked if I would keep an eye on you. I know you're a good boy, and I don't want to see you get into any trouble!"

Wow, I said to myself. *It's happening again! That's what Mommy would say!*

Ring, ring, went the second bell.

Whew! I made it in time!

22

My homeroom teacher, Ms. Workman, greeted all her students at the door. "Good morning!" she said to each of us, but there was one surprise that was just for me. She pulled me to the side.

What have I done? I wondered. *Am I in trouble already—on the first day of school?*

Ms. Workman leaned down to me and said, "Your mother called me right after I got to work this morning."

Uh oh, I thought. *What had my mommy said?*

"Alex," the teacher said."

She even knows my name, I thought.

"Your mother tells me that you help her around the house. She says you make the beds. She says you take out the garbage, sweep the floors, and help your brother and sister get dressed. I think that's very sweet of you."

"Thank you, ma'am," I said. *I must not be in trouble after all!*

But Ms. Workman wasn't finished. "Your mother also asked me to keep an eye on you," she said with a smile. "That's why I want you to sit beside my desk for the whole school year!"

Oh no, I thought. *I'll never make new friends. I'll be picked on all year long.*

Then the teacher told me there was another reason that she wanted me to sit in front. A few of the other boys in class didn't follow rules as well as I did. I would be a great example for the others, she explained. "Your teacher from your old school said I was so lucky to have you in my class!"

It went on like that all day. In every single class, someone pulled me aside to say they had their eye on me. "Stay out of trouble, Alex," everybody said. It was like I had my mommy right there with me everywhere I turned!

Or was it my imagination?

Hanging with Alvin and Reggie in the Gym

Ring, ring, went the bell for gym. My best buddies, Alvin and Reggie from my old school, would be in that class with me. We were all starting out at our new school together!

Alvin loved to play pranks. He loved telling jokes that would make my stomach hurt because I laughed so hard. There was one funny prank that I never will forget. After I sprained my ankle while playing basketball, he sneaked up behind me with a fake rubber snake. He knew I couldn't run away, and he laughed and laughed.

He had a big family, and they were so much fun. Alvin's mother was Mrs. Bezzie, and she would cook for all the kids in the neighborhood. Fried chicken! Mac and cheese! Sweet potato pie! She made shrimp and fried rice and the best sauces that I have ever tasted. I would take my brother and sister with me to Alvin's house to play and eat. It was very easy to blend in with the crowd. There are so many people who lived at Alvin's house and so many kids who came to play!

Now, Reggie, on the other hand, was a different kind of buddy. Reggie loved adventures. He knew all kinds of games. One day, when the power went out in my apartment, Reggie and Alvin came over with their flashlights to play hide-and-seek. On another day, after a big storm, we made cardboard boats and raced them in the puddles. Oh boy! Was that ever fun!

Reggie had all kinds of cool stuff, like the brand-new sneakers he got every week. He had new suits for church. He had the latest Xbox and a big toy-car collection—things that most of us could not afford to have. But Reggie loved to share!

In the gym, I asked my friends how their first day was going. Alvin told us he got pranked—and with his own fake mouse! Here is how it happened. A kid hid the mouse in Alvin's book bag, and when Alvin opened up the bag to get his notebook, out came that big, furry rodent! Alvin's scream was so loud that they could hear him in the parking lot.

We laughed so hard that we were crying. Then it got even better! The person who pranked Alvin was the shy and quiet girl who sat at the desk behind him. That just made our day!

I'm Not in Trouble Yet!

Ring, ring! It was our last class of the day! At the door to my classroom, I saw the principal, Mrs. McCants, talking to my science teacher. I already liked this teacher, whose name was Mrs. Lee. Mrs. Lee was tall. She had a pretty smile.

"Is that him?" Mrs. McCants asked my teacher when I walked into the room.

What did I do now? I thought. *Why is the principal looking at me that way? She doesn't even know me! I'm a new kid at this school!*

That is when it happened. Principal McCants wiggled her finger at me to come out into the hall.

Danger! Danger! I thought. Something bad was up! I walked close—but not too close.

I got another finger wiggle.

Slowly—very slowly—I walked a little closer. I was so scared that I was sweating.

She leaned down and whispered, "Ms. Beverly's a friend of mine. She asked me yesterday to keep an eye on you. She said you are a good boy and that she didn't want you to get into any trouble." Then she gave me the kind of look my mommy always gave me. It was a look that made you feel like you'd done something that you hadn't. But you would take the blame so that your mommy wouldn't look at you that way. A kid might stand out in the rain—without an umbrella, too—for a whole five minutes to avoid that look.

Principal McCants patted me on the shoulder, smiled, and said, "You have a good day, Alex."

Wow, I said to myself. Even my new principal was in on the act! Could it be really true? Could my mommy really be everywhere I went? Had I been seeing Mommy all day long?

Ring, ring, went the second bell. I scooted past Mrs. Lee to find a seat. I didn't want to bring even *more* attention to myself.

"Will all students please stand up?" asked the teacher.

Uh-oh. What now? I thought. Sometimes it meant trouble when a teacher asked the class to stand.

Then Mrs. Lee continued. "I have decided to assign seats in alphabetical order."

This is bad, I thought. The first seat was right next to her desk, and my name started with an *A.* Sweating, I tried to think of ways to keep Mrs. Lee from calling out my name. Maybe I could ask to go to the restroom? Nah! Way too obvious. So instead, I slowly started walking to the back of the room, hoping someone else's name started with an *A* like mine. Maybe they'd be first.

As I hid behind two tall kids, Mrs. Lee began to call the roll. "The first name on the roll is . . ."

Please! Don't let it be me, I thought.

"Alex," she continued, finishing the sentence. "Come on up here, Alex, and please take your seat!"

Bummer! I sat down in my new seat right beside the teacher's desk.

After everyone was seated, she turned to me and winked. "I know who you are," she whispered with a smile. "I put you by me on purpose. You're little Alex—Ms. Beverly's son! I spoke with your mother this morning over the telephone, and she said to please make sure that I keep an eye on you."

Then it hit me once again. It was like a light bulb had come on inside my head. She was speaking the same words that I'd heard all day. It was like my mommy was sitting right there with me!

Finally! The End of a Long Day

*R*ing, ring! That was the bell that meant the school day was almost over. I had gotten through the first day of the third grade! And, boy, what an exciting day it had been. I could hardly wait to meet up with Alvin and Reggie. I was sure they had some good stories they could tell me about their classes.

Ring, ring, went the second bell.

"School's out!" some kid shouted.

Mrs. Lee stood up from her desk. "Make sure you have all your belongings and pick up any trash around your desk," she said. She began to line us up in the order she had seated us. Then she calmly walked toward me and leaned down with a smile. "Not you, Alex," she said. "You will walk behind the line with me."

Bummer. This can't be happening, I thought. *Why me? What will the others think?* I sat at my desk until all the other students had walked by.

Mrs. Lee then turned to me and said, "Now Alex, get in line!" She closely followed me to the bus ramp. Jokingly, she said, "Let your mother know that I made sure you didn't get into any trouble on your first day."

"Yes ma'am," I replied.

Later, I was running at top speed to make it onto the bus when I was spotted by Principal McCants. You'd better believe that stopped me right there in my tracks! *Squeak* was the sound my sneakers made as I came to a stop.

"Hey! You are Alex, right?" she asked.

"Yes ma'am," I replied.

"There is no running on the bus ramp."

"Yes ma'am. It won't happen again!"

"Besides," she said, "I told Ms. Beverly I was going to keep an eye on you today!"

"Yes ma'am," I replied.

"Tell your mother I said hello!"

"Yes ma'am." I walked away—very slowly.

The Bus Pulls Away from School

I could see Alvin and Reggie at the front of the line. They were going to get some of the best seats! They were laughing with some other kids. That meant I was missing some of Alvin's jokes. I was supposed to be up there with them, joking with my buddies and making new friends too.

That's it, I told myself. *I can't take it anymore!* Everyone else would get the good seats, and I'd get stuck somewhere far away from my two best buddies.

Zoom! I took off running toward the front of the line. I made it past Ms. Oliver, the watchful bus attendant. Score! Before she could turn around and see me, I slid in behind my friends.

Some of the other kids were laughing at my trick. One of them was Angie from my apartment building. She turned to me and said, "On Saturday, I heard your mommy and my mommy talking. Your mommy sounded sad."

That's not good, I thought. "What did she say?" I asked.

"Your mommy said she wished that she could be around to make sure you have had a good day at your new school. But I told her not to worry. I told her *I'd* be here! I'd keep an eye on you! I told her I was starting fifth grade—which means I'm almost all grown-up. I've been watching you today, and I saw the teachers watching too. Your mommy certainly made sure there were lots of eyes on you!"

"**W**ow," I said. "I knew that there was something strange about this day! It was almost like I was seeing Mommy all day long!"

Angie laughed, and then it was my turn to get on the bus. Alvin and Reggie had already gotten on and were looking for good seats.

Then Ms. Oliver called out for me to stop.

Had she seen me sneaking into the line behind my buddies? I was sure I was in trouble now. And I'd almost made it to the end of the day!

Ms. Oliver leaned down next to me. "Hello!" she said. "Did you have a good day at school? Since I promised your mother I'd keep an eye on you, I wanted to make sure."

"Thank you, ma'am. I did." *Phew.* I had not been caught! Everything was good. I hurried to find a seat by my buddies.

Finally, Ms. Oliver got on the bus, and the bus driver shut the door. *Shhh* was the sound of the doors closing.

Alvin, Reggie, and I were small enough to fit onto one seat. We talked about the kids we'd met. We talked about our teachers. We talked about the GIANT cheeseburgers and the french fries we got to eat for lunch. Yum. We talked about the way we won at basketball because we each knew the others' moves.

Then before we knew it, we heard shhhhh as the bus doors opened. We were already at our stop!

As each kid got off, we said goodbye to Ms. Oliver and the driver, Ms. O'Keefe. When it was my turn to get off, the driver tapped me on the shoulder. "I saw you dip into the line in front of the other kids," she said. "I should have made you go back to the end of the line."

My heart began to race. Busted after all!

She went on to say, "Since I told your mother I'd keep an eye on you, I let you stay up front with your friends—just once. But remember that I'm watching!"

Now I felt really awful about the way I'd been so sneaky. "I'm sorry, Ms. O'Keefe. I won't do it again."

"You'd better not." She gave me a big smile to let me know she was joking. "Now get outta here, you little rascal."

Mrs. Baxter's store

36

Cookies and a Collision

After waving bye to my buddies, I stopped by the corner store. I made a beeline to the candy and cookie aisle. I counted out the change in my pocket. Five . . . ten . . . fifteen . . . twenty-five! I had twenty-five cents, just enough to buy three cookies *and* three pieces of candy for my brother, my sister, and myself.

At the counter, Mrs. Baxter, the store owner, watched me with a big smile on her face. "Well?" she asked.

I looked at her, confused. "Well, *what*, Mrs. Baxter?"

"Well, did you have a good day at school?"

"Oh, yes ma'am, Mrs. Baxter. I had a great day!"

"That's good to hear!" she said. "You know, Ms. Beverly called right before you came into the store this morning, and she said to me, 'Mrs. Baxter, please make sure Alex gets in and out of the store and hurries to the bus stop. I don't want him to miss the bus and be late on the first day of school!' I told your mother, Alex, that I would keep an eye on you."

So *that's* why Mrs. Baxter had hurried me out of the store!

"Your mother also said to tell you to go to Mrs. Bezzie's house and stay until she gets off from work. Your brother and sister are already there."

I paid for my stuff. "Yes ma'am, Mrs. Baxter. Thank you. Have a good day!" I said. I left for my apartment to change out of my school clothes before heading to Mrs. Bezzie's.

I was running fast when—*boom*—I ran into Mrs. Simpkins and the twins. "Sorry, Mrs. Simpkins!"

She just laughed and said, "Boy, you almost knocked a hole in my side! So, where is the fire, Alex?"

By then, the twins were laughing too!

I felt so embarrassed. "Oh, no ma'am! No fire! I was just going to change out of my school clothes."

Mrs. Simpkins smiled. "This morning, I saw your mother, and she asked me to keep an eye on you if I saw you after school."

Mrs. Simpkins too?

She winked. "Well, Alex, it was nice *running into you* today!"

The twins howled with laughter, then their mom led them away.

I stood there for a little while and thought about what I'd heard. Could it still be happening? Could I really be seeing Mommy ALL DAY LONG? I shook it off and ran to the elevators.

As soon as I got off on my floor, before I could stick my key into the apartment door, I heard someone calling.

Going to Mrs. Bezzie's House

"Alex is that you?" It was Mrs. Jones, the "grandmother" with the treats.

"Yes, Mrs. Jones," I said.

She made her way toward me. "How was school today?"

"School was great!" I answered.

"I saw your mother in the lobby when she was on her way to work. I said I'd look after you, your brother, and your sister until she got home. She said, 'That's all right this time, Mrs. Jones. I've already made some plans for a friend to keep them at her house. But thank you for volunteering!' I told her I'd be glad to help out anytime. Sooo, Alex . . ." Mrs. Jones raised her eyebrows at me. "Why are you going into the apartment when you're supposed to be somewhere else?"

"I was going to change out of my school clothes," I replied.

"Okay, that's a smart boy! Well, let the old lady go now. I need to check those pots I left on the stove." She headed down the hall. "Yes, I told your mother that I would keep an eye on you!"

All I could do was laugh as I opened my apartment door. Quickly, I changed my clothes and left. I did not forget my book bag so I could do my homework.

Down the elevator I went.

As I reached the lobby, I ran to the door—but stopped. I did *not* want a collision with another neighbor. After making sure the coast was clear, I took off running. *Zoom!* I was off to Mrs. Bezzie's house to see my brother and my sister and, of course, my best buddy, Alvin.

Fun at Mrs. Bezzie's House and the Walk Home

As I ran, I thought about my first day at the new school and about Mrs. Bezzie's yummy Southern cooking. Deep-fried chicken! Mashed potatoes! Meatloaf, mushroom rice, collard greens, ham, fish, and hot apple pie! When I got closer to her front porch, I could already smell the food. *Ding-dong!* I rang the bell, and can you guess who came to the door?

It was my buddy Alvin! "Come on in, boy, with your dirty face!" he would always joke.

I would always say, "So glad to see you, Alvin, and your toenail head." Both of us would laugh.

Once inside, I saw my little brother and sister playing with the younger kids. They both ran to hug me, and I whispered in their ears, "I've got something for you, but it's for after dinner."

"Go wash up. It's time to eat!" said Mrs. Bezzie.

I could hardly wait!

After we were seated, Alvin and I got up to help serve the drinks, and I had an idea. I had been hoping all day long to get Alvin with a prank, and now I had my chance.

In my bookbag, I kept a pack of thumbtacks that had been on our list of things to buy for school. Now, I placed some thumbtacks under Alvin's cushion, and when he sat back down, he jumped clear to the ceiling. Everybody laughed until they were in tears.

Even Alvin laughed! "You got me, Alex! Good one!"

After dinner, which came complete with corny jokes from Alvin, it was time for homework. Mrs. Bezzie walked over to the spot where we were working. "How was dinner, Alex?"

I felt something rising in my throat. *Burp!* "Mrs. Bezzie, I'm so sorry!" I told her, embarrassed.

"That's nasty," said one of Alvin's little sisters, and everybody giggled.

Then I finally answered Mrs. Bezzie. "Your food always tastes delicious!"

Ding-dong! Mrs. Bezzie opened the door, and there was Mommy. My brother and sister ran to her, excited.

"We missed you!" my sister said.

I slowly walked up to my mommy and saw her sheepish smile.

"Well, Alex, how was your day today?" she asked.

All I could do was laugh. I gave her a big hug. "School was great—but I think you know that already."

She grinned at me again. "You can tell me all about it when we get home."

We all thanked Mrs. Bezzie.

As I walked home with my family, I thought about my day. Each piece of advice I got from every person I ran into was something Mommy would have said. It was like seeing Mommy all day long!

CPSIA information can be obtained
at www.ICGtesting.com
Printed in the USA
LVHW070716270423
745223LV00002B/2

9 780578 911861